Old Taynuilt
Guthrie Hutton

GW00568258

Ben Cruachan, one of Scotland's most majestic mountains, stands sentinel over Taynuilt in this early twentieth century view.

Erected in 1805, and seen here about 100 years later, the monument at Taynuilt is believed to have been the first in Britain to honour Lord Nelson. The Lorn Furnace workmen put it up using a huge standing stone from Airds.

© Guthrie Hutton, 2013
First published in the United Kingdom, 2013, by Stenlake Publishing Ltd.
www.stenlake.co.uk
ISBN 9781840336276

The publishers regret that they cannot supply copies of any pictures featured in this book.

Acknowledgements

In the mid-1960s my mother lived at Taynuilt and so, on most weekends, my sister and I jumped into my little van and drove up from Glasgow. We coped with all weathers, apart from one morning when we slid off the road near Inveraray, side-swiping telegraph pole. That was scary, especially for my sister – the pole was on her side – but on all other occasions we enjoyed swapping city stresses for the shores of Loch Etive. Taynuilt was special then and it has been a real pleasure to revive the memories of those days by compiling this little book. I have been assisted in this endeavour by my sister, who was drawn back to Argyll many years ago and was huge help both with her own memories and looking after me on my travels. Most of the pictures have come from the collection of my friend Ian Kennedy who also shared ideas. Murray and Mairead Sim and Evelyn and Catriona Campbell were a great help answering questions and adding memories. am grateful to them and to Taynuilt Golf Club for permission to use the pictures on page 29. The resources of the Mitchell Library, Glasgow, and the Oban Library also proved invaluable.

Further Reading
The books listed below were used by the author during his research. None are available from Stenlake Publishing; please contact your local bookshop or reference library

Atkinson, Graham, *J. & A. Gardner & Co. Ltd.*, 2002.
Duckworth, C., and Langmuir, G., *Clyde River and Other Steamers*, 1946.
Grimble, Augustus, *The Salmon Rivers of Scotland*, 1900.
Haldane, A. R. B, *The Drove Roads of Scotland*, 1952.
MacKay, James A., *Scottish Post Offices*, 1980s.
MacLean, Allan, *Telford's Highland Churches*, 1989.

Stell, G. P., and Hay G. D., *Bonawe Iron Furnace*, 1984.
Taynuilt S. W. R. I., *Taynuilt: Our History*, 1966 (+ revisions).
Thomas, John, *The Callander & Oban Railway*, 1966.
Walker, Frank Arneil, *The Buildings of Scotland: Argyll & Bute*, 2000.
Weir, Marie, *Ferries in Scotland*, 1988.
Wendling, Walter, *Ferry Tales of Argyll and the Western Isles*, 1996.

Introduction

Gaelic place names can sometimes be tricky to define, but not Taynuilt, it means house (taigh) by the stream (an uillt), but while the name's meaning is clear, the identity of the original house is less so although the hotel, or an early version of it, is the most likely candidate.

Over time Taynuilt spread beyond the limits of that single house to become the all-embracing name for a collection of small settlements including Ichrachan, Kirkton, Bonawe, Brochroy, Hafton and Airds. It also developed into a key location on the roads that crossed the county between east and west, and north and south by way of the Bonawe Ferry, and it might have remained as just another village at a crossroads had it not been for two important developments. The first came in the 1750s when a company from the English Lake District set up a furnace for smelting iron. It burned charcoal and was small compared to the huge hot-blast furnaces of the nineteenth century, but it provided employment for many people, both at the smelter and burning charcoal in woodlands spread over a wide area. The effects of coppicing trees for charcoal burning can still be seen in local woods where another industry, the making of birch brooms for use in steel mills, thrived in the early years of the twentieth century.

The furnace changed Taynuilt from what it might have been by making it into a place of industry in an area that was otherwise dominated by large estates and a rural economy. Crofting, farming, forestry and salmon fishing occupied many people, but the connection with heavy industry was maintained by quarrying, an activity that also provided employment for people in Taynuilt even though the largest quarry was on the other side of the loch.

Economic realities eventually defeated the furnace just before the next big development for Taynuilt, the arrival of the railway. At that time roads were poor, so the railway, quicker and able to carry heavier loads, began to transform the village. The station was sited close to the existing core of the community; the church, school and hotel, and with shops and houses being built in close proximity a recognisable village street took shape. The railway also made it easier for people to visit the area and take part in country pursuits like walking and fishing.

With the hotel in the background, the south end of the village street is seen here about 1907.

Tourism developed in other ways too, as trips that combined horse-drawn coaches with loch steamers and railway trains attracted sightseers to the area. Road improvements in the middle years of the twentieth century made travelling easier for more people, but also made it possible for them to go further and faster, and be more fickle in deciding where to stop. Reasons for them to swing into Taynuilt developed in the 1970s and 80s as visitor attractions were established, one of which, as if to bring the wheel full circle, was the Bonawe Ironworks, back in business, but this time as an ancient monument, contributing to a tourist industry that is as vital to the local economy as iron once was.

Taynuilt, and all its satellites, is set amongst some spectacular geographical features one of which, Ben Cruachan, is seen in this view looking east from Ichrachan. It is an imposing mountain with more than one peak. The one facing the village, Stob Dearg, sometimes referred to as the 'Taynuilt Peak', 72 feet (22 metres) lower than the summit, which is 3,694 feet (1126 metres) high. As with so many things in the Highlands, the mountain has a legend. The story goes that a cailleach (an old woman) guarded a spring on the summit and at sunset she had to place a stone over it, but on one fateful evening fell asleep. When she awoke the spring had overflowed, flooding the valley below the mountain and forming Loch Awe, which burst through the gap between the hills thus also making the Pass of Brander and the River Awe. The cailleach's reward for creating this scenic magnificence was to be turned to stone.

chrachan again occupies the foreground of this view looking west across the roof of Springbank House to Loch Etive, one of Scotland's most varied and eautiful lochs. Going west from Taynuilt the loch's southern shores are wooded and gently sloping, those to the north, more rugged, but to the east of aynuilt the loch also turns north into wild mountainous country that only intrepid foot travellers and those on the water ever see. Of course it has a gend, that of Deirdre of the Sorrows, a beautiful young woman from Ulster who eloped with her lover, Naoise, one of the three sons of Uisneach. For time, they lived beside Loch Etive guarded by Naoise's brothers, but were tricked into returning to Ireland by Conchobar mac Nessa, King of Ulster, ie man to whom Deirdre was betrothed. There was a fight, Naoise was killed, and the king took the unhappy Deirdre as his wife. Inevitably the marriage iled, and Deirdre killed herself or died of a broken heart. Either way the story has a melancholy ending as is often the way with Celtic tales.

5

The area's array of impressive natural features also includes the River Awe, which although being only four miles long, follows a dramatic course from Loch Awe to Loch Etive that includes the forbidding defile of the Pass of Brander. The river presented a formidable barrier to early travellers. It could be forded, with difficulty, in dry seasons and there may have been an early bridge, but it was not until the three-arched bridge was completed in 1779 that a reliable road could be made between Oban and Dalmally. During construction, one pier of the bridge was damaged in a flood and in 1992 another flood swept away all but the arch on the Taynuilt side. The bridge featured in a film, *The Bridal Path*, but by that time, 1959, it was no longer the main crossing having been superseded by the single span concrete bridge seen in the foreground of this picture. Designed by Sir Frank Mears, it was completed in 193 as part of more general road improvements throughout the Highland counties.

o the men building the Callander and Oban Railway line, the River Awe and the Pass of Brander represented two of their biggest challenges. The road lready occupied a strip of ground through the pass, so the railway had to carve a new route out of the steep side of Ben Cruachan. The mountain was lso littered with loose boulders that clung precariously to the slopes. Many of these were cleared and crushed for use in concrete, but countless others emained, just waiting to tumble down the mountain onto the rails. To counteract this danger a boulder screen consisting of wires stretched on poles was nstalled above the line. The idea was that falling boulders would break the wire and set off a signal to warn trains that the track could be blocked. In a ind the wires made a musical sound, so the arrangement became known as Anderson's piano, after the company secretary, John Anderson. At the west nd of the pass the line crossed the river on this fine lattice girder viaduct.

With the whole of Loch Awe behind it, the Awe is a swift, strong river. It is seen here at the west end of the Pass of Brander, where it began to fall away from the level of the loch. Known to anglers as the Brander Pool, the highest point on the river where they could hook a salmon, this was also the location selected in the early 1960s for a hydroelectric barrage. Construction was well under way in February 1962 when the coffer-dam protecting the site, and a quantity of tools and heavy equipment were overwhelmed in a flood. With their shuttering floating in Loch Etive, the contractors, Mitchell Construction of Glasgow, had little choice but to repair the damage and carry on, while the construction workers hoped to find salmon trapped in the workings when they were pumped out. Although a fish pass was incorporated into the structure, the flow of water and behaviour of the salmon were affected, and attempts have since been made to mimic natural seasonal flows and improve the fishery.

As if one river isn't enough, Taynuilt has two, both following courses down the east side of the village. The second of these, the River Nant, is seen here flowing past the crofting township of Ichrachan in a picture from the 1890s. The houses are all still thatched in a style typical of Argyll where the roofs overlap the wall head, unlike Hebridean houses where the thatch often sat on top of the wall. Some evolution of building style is evident with some houses constructed with gable ends and some with hipped, or piended roofs. A peat stack shows that the traditional fuel of the Highlands has not yet been supplanted by coal. Ichrachan sat at the crossroads of the direct route between the Bonawe Ferry and Loch Awe, by way of Glen Nant.

Glen Nant became part of a tourist route in Victorian times when coaches like this splendid four-in-hand brought people to enjoy the natural beauties of the glen. The trip they were on, described at the time as 'a wee gem of a tour' took them through the glen to Loch Awe where they joined a steamer for a sail before returning to Oban by rail. The road through the glen was narrow and steeply graded, twisting and turning on precarious-looking engineering that the coach drivers probably regarded as all in a day's work, while the visitors will have been thrilled by the frisson of danger and charmed by the glen's loveliness. One of the glen's principal attractions was the waterfall known as Tailor's Leap, so named because a tailor, who had been attending an illicit still, was discovered by excise men and escaped his pursuers by leaping from rock to rock across the river.

A coach, in the top left hand corner of this picture, has stopped beside the Tailor's Leap, which has been spanned by little rickety-looking footbridges that he more intrepid visitors could use to get a closer view of the tumbling water. The falls are less impressive than they once were because the Nant was arnessed in the early 1960s for a hydroelectric scheme. Loch Nant, the source of the river and the catchment for numerous little burns that tumble into his natural basin, was trebled in size by the construction of a dam. Water from the loch was fed by way of a tunnel, eight feet in diameter and 3,700 feet ong, to an underground power station, beside Loch Awe. Opened in 1963, it is relatively small, initially designed to produce about 27 million units of lectricity annually, and although entirely self-contained is regarded as being part of the overall scheme that includes the impressive pump-storage ydroelectric station dug into the side of Ben Cruachan.

The Taynuilt Hotel, seen here with one of the Glen Nant coaches outside, has at its core an eighteenth century inn. It faces the main road to and from Oban but also sits at the junction of the route between the Bonawe Ferry and Oban by way of Glen Lonan, a road preferred by drovers. Before the main road was improved, the route to the east through the Pass of Brander could be difficult, thus making the road through Glen Nant to the ferry across Loch Awe to Portsonachan a preferred route for some travellers. In those days, before road vehicles made people think differently, ferries were an accepted part of travel and more numerous. Some early travellers stopped at the Taynuilt Inn: Dorothy Wordsworth, along with her brother William and fellow poet Samuel Coleridge, found it very congenial in 1803 with good breakfasts, excellent supper, and, including accommodation for their horses, all at a modest cost. A decade or so later another traveller described it as 'a vile pot house', a change that can perhaps be put down to the passage of time or a bad temper.

n the late nineteenth and early twentieth centuries the hotel leased fishing rights on the River Awe from the Duke of Argyll and attracted customers with 'splendid salmon angling free to visitors'. Guests will have paid for such an offer somehow, but the hotel was still offering moderate terms in the early 930s when one holidaymaker sent this picture postcard to a friend. They found that the weather was 'nothing to complain of', but did seem irked because he Oban sales had started and the roads were busy. The much-improved main road had placed the hotel in an ideal position to pick up passing trade rom motorists, as is evident from the car that has stopped outside the hotel. Petrol pumps and a garage, with cars for hire, occupy the stabling where)orothy Wordsworth and her companions sheltered their horses for the night. The hotel was also keen to promote the outstanding scenery of the local rea, free access to sea trout fishing on Loch Etive and electric light, which did not arrive for the bulk of the village until 1948.

The hotel and its outbuildings are in the left foreground of this early twentieth century view of the village from the south. In the centre of the picture is the school. There had been a village school for at least 100 years before Lady Campbell of Lochnell paid for a parish school in 1834, but following the Education Act of 1872 such establishments were taken over by school boards. A new Taynuilt school was built in the 1890s, subsequently extended, augmented with a hut (known in official circles as a mobile classroom) and replaced by a new building in January 1988. Schools were one of a number of civic functions run (quoad civilia) by parishes and for Taynuilt, that was Ardchattan Parish, although after 1829, church-only affairs came under a new quoad sacra parish of Muckairn. An earlier parish, known as Killespickerill, had formerly held sway in Muckairn and a pre-Reformation church occupied a site just to the south of the new church, seen here to the right of the school.

he church, built in 1828/29, incorporates a number of features (like the windows and bellcote) of what are known as 'parliamentary churches'. In 1824 arliament approved funds to help the Established Church of Scotland extend its reach in the Highlands by erecting new churches and manses. The job of esigning and building these was given to the Commissioners of Highland Roads and Bridges, and they delegated it to their chief surveyor, Thomas Telford. e in turn got his local surveyors to produce designs, which were then modified to create a standard building that could be erected at a known cost, modified nly by local conditions. At Taynuilt, the cost of the new church was met by General Campbell of Lochnell, which helps to explain why it does not conform the standard pattern. Another curiosity is that it incorporates in the south wall an ancient (possibly thirteenth century) fertility stone known, in Gaelic, as sile-na-gcioc. The manse, a two-storey house was, unlike the church, paid for out of government funds and built to the standard design.

Despite being closer to the camera, the buildings in this picture of Taynuilt, taken from the south, look diminutive compared to the prominent scar of Bonawe Quarry on the far side of Loch Etive. The Glen Lonan road is seen winding out of the village on the left. The picture was taken in 1932, but this print of it was published as postcard during the Second World War with a quote from a speech delivered in 1941 by the Prime Minister, Winston Churchill, printed on the back. Also written on the back is a message that hints at some kind of training exercise: 'Sleep in field at back of church' and 'Take food in annex of school' – very mysterious, but not clandestine! Since this picture was taken, and especially since the Second World War, a lot of new houses (including a number of council houses) have been built, changing the look of this scene and others throughout the village.

et amongst wooded grounds further up the glen was a delightful property built in 1906 – 1908 as Barguillean House and later renamed Lonan House. he architect was Robert S. Lorimer, one of the most significant exponents of the Arts and Crafts style in Scotland. His work included Ardkinglas House t the head of Loch Fyne and the restoration of nearby Dunderave Castle, a combination of new build and restoration of older properties that was typical f the range of work he undertook, and which extended to designing the furnishing and fittings for some interiors. He received a knighthood for his work n the Thistle Chapel at St Giles Cathedral in Edinburgh, completed in 1911. After the First World War he designed a number of war memorials, war rave cemeteries and the Scottish National War Memorial at Edinburgh Castle. This picture of Lonan House shows it soon after conversion to a hotel.

Cnocrannoch, on the main road to the west of the Taynuilt Hotel, was one of many houses in the village where, from time to time, accommodation ha been provided for visitors. Styled as a 'board residence', its proprietor encapsulated the B & B owners' agony of trying to make the most of a short seaso when they sent this card in 1939 to a prospective customer in London. The message reads: 'sorry, I have made a mistake with dates and I can now tak you on 16th August. If suitable to you now, will be glad of an early reply'. There were of course no e-mails in those days, so in the absence of a telephone a postcard would have been the surest way to get a quick response.

On the north side of the main road, across from Cnocrannoch, was the Taynuilt Store, seen here in a late nineteenth or early twentieth century picture. At the time it was owned and run by Donald McNiven, who can be seen outside the door resplendent in a large apron wrapped around his equally ample figure. It was a general store that, judging by the variety of shapes that can be seen through the windows, included a wide range of goods. It is thought that the building dated from at least the middle of the nineteenth century and was thus in existence before the opening of the railway. This suggests that, had the station not been sited where it was, Taynuilt might have developed along the main road rather than in the way that it did. Mr McNiven sold the store in 1916 to Donald Gillies who ran it for many years, but without water or sanitation, the building was latterly used as a byre and steading before being demolished in 1972.

The north/south road through the village is seen here in a picture taken a year or two perhaps either side of 1900. The cottages were situated close to the junction with the main road and the photographer has populated his picture of them with some men. One looks like a postman, two could just have been around or there to help the one man whose occupation is not in doubt, the thatcher. There was apparently a local thatcher who had only one leg – it's not clear from the picture, but it could be him up the ladder. It is equally unclear what the thatch is made of, but heather, rushes, bracken or straw were all used. Whatever the material, the neatly-finished roof, roped to the gable wall and weighted with poles, is a testament to the man's skill. The cottage at the far end, with a porch, appears to have a shop sign beside the door and for over 100 years the same family ran a cobbler's and later, a sweet shop that only ceased trading in 2004. By that time the appearance of these buildings had been significantly altered.

he thatched cottages on the facing page are unrecognisable as the dormer windowed houses on the left of this picture dating from 1939. The road too as been transformed from the roughly surfaced, ill-defined track to the neatly-ordered, kerb-lined thoroughfare seen here. On the right is a telephone iosk, which will have been installed not long before the picture was taken. These distinctive items of street furniture had gone through a number of evelopmental phases before a design was selected as the one to be set up throughout the country after the mid-1930s. They became a symbol of Britain, n almost inseparable feature of town and country, but were not always red. In rural areas, where the bright colour might have been intrusive, the boxes ere sometimes painted grey with red glazing bars, as appears to be the case with this one in Taynuilt. The phone box, painted red, became such a feature f the village that when it was threatened with removal a local campaign was mounted to save it.

With his sack slung over his shoulder, a postman trudges past Aros House in 1931. There had been a post office at Bonawe since the mid-1770s, but closed in October 1865, an operational period that broadly echoed that of the ironworks. For the village, this wasn't so much a closure, as a transfe because the opening of Taynuilt's post office coincided with the demise of the one at Bonawe. Initially an independent sub-office, it was upgraded in 188 to the status of railway sub-office, which meant that some or all of the mail going through it was received from a travelling post office without having t go through a head office. Such organisational niceties were probably lost on most people who just wanted to be able to send and receive mail, buy stamp and postal orders, and use the savings bank. On the road beside the postie is what looks like a recent deposit of horse droppings, a bounty of free manu that, had it been in a city, would surely have been shovelled up by someone for their roses.

he *New Statistical Account*, written in the early 1840s, contains an intriguing reference to the inns of Muckairn Parish. It states that there are two, and continues: 'one of which is necessary, while the other, it is believed might be dispensed with, without inconvenience'. The author of the account was a inister and his antipathy to the inns might have had something to do with a dislike of the demon drink. If this is correct he would have approved of aynuilt's Temperance Hotel, seen in this picture from 1909. The Temperance movement began in Scotland around the 1830s and by the middle of the ntury a number of organisations dedicated to promoting abstinence had come into existence. To this was added an informal network of temperance otels where travellers could find sanctuary from the temptations on offer at licensed establishments. A temptation that local boys found hard to resist as an orchard in front of the house, while behind it is the monument to Lord Nelson, a man not known for eschewing the odd tot of rum.

The village shops were clustered in the vicinity of the railway station, as this early twentieth century picture shows. Laroch, the large house to the left of centre with a woman, children and pram outside, was the location of another shop known as the Taynuilt Stores, run at the time by A. McInnes. evidently stocked fishing tackle amongst a variety of other goods. In the neighbouring building Mr. Campbell sold general merchandise and meat. Across the road was the Argyle Stores, which at times under the one roof hosted the post office and dealt in merchandise ranging from hardware to newspaper In the 1950s, when he wrote the *Third Statistical Account*, the Rev. Murdo MacDonald recorded that there were nine shops in the village: two butchers, two grocers, two hardware shops, one drapery, a confectioner and a tea room. The latter was the Robin's Nest, which occupied the former shop in the Laroc House building and has since become something of a village institution.

War may have been looming, but there is no hint of the tension gripping Europe in this picture of unhurried everyday life taken in 1939. The road leading to the station is seen on the right, behind it are the petrol pumps of the Taynuilt Garage and beyond them, the Argyle Stores. A feature of the village for many years, the Argyle Stores was to undergo a big change in June 1942 when it became a retail branch of the Scottish Co-operative Wholesale Society (SCWS). Historically the SCWS supplied goods to the many co-op retail societies around the country, but the fact that some places had no retail society troubled the co-op movement. Many of these so-called 'deserts' were in the north of Scotland where the SCWS began a process of opening retail stores just before the First World War. Eighteen had been established by the outbreak of the Second World War, which seemed to act as some sort of catalyst because, while the war was on, over 50 stores were opened, including the one at Taynuilt.

Taynuilt's tourist trade and communications with the wider world were transformed in June 1880 when the final section of the Callander & Oban Railway between Dalmally and Oban was opened. The story of the line began over thirty years earlier when the Scottish Central Railway, which ran between Perth and Greenhill, near Bonnybridge in Stirlingshire, was built. A branch from Dunblane to Callander was completed in 1858 and a proposal to extend this all the way to Oban was agreed in 1864, only a few months before the Scottish Central was taken over by the great Caledonian Railway. The 'Caley' had ambitions to extend its influence north and south, and was unenthusiastic about the proposed line to the west, but the Callander & Oban Railway Company appointed a new man, John Anderson, to run its affairs, and it was his drive and determination that saw work begin in October 1866 and advance steadily westward: to Killin by 1870, Tyndrum, 1873, Dalmally, 1877 and finally, triumphantly, Oban (and Taynuilt) by 1880.

Despite their misgivings, the Caledonian Railway Company operated the line up to the railway amalgamations of 1923 when it became the preserve of the London, Midland & Scottish Railway (LMS). The Callander & Oban continued to own the infrastructure and remained as an independent entity until it too was absorbed by the LMS, whose advertising notices are still displayed in this picture from 1950, two years after the railways were nationalised in 1948. The line going east from Crianlarich would have closed under the 'Beeching' cuts of the 1960s had a landslide not brought it to a premature end, but the Oban section remained open, using a spur to the West Highland line at Crianlarich. Taynuilt became an unmanned station in 1988, but a further proposal to demolish the historic wooden building was thwarted by the community council who managed to get it designated as a B-listed structure. It remained closed and boarded up, but in September 2000, while plans to make it into a heritage centre were being developed, vandals burned it to the ground.

In the century and more that has passed since a photographer lined up this picture across the River Nant, tree growth has obscured the view. Facing the camera is the house known as Forest Bank, while half-hidden in the trees to the right is the village hall. It was built in 1905 to the designs of Oban architect George Woulfe Brenan and must have been very new when the picture was taken, also in 1905. Following its opening the hall has been at the centre of village social life. With a stage, and able to accommodate audiences of up to 150 people, it has hosted plays by the local amateur dramatic society, film shows and a variety of ceremonies. Ceilidhs, dances and children's parties were always popular as was the annual flower and vegetable show staged by the Taynuilt Horticultural Society following its formation in 1928.

f the number of courses set up in the area during the twentieth century is taken as a measure, Taynuilt must be one of golf's leading centres, but while hree opened, two were short-lived. The first of these, seen in these pictures from 1912, was in existence by 1910. The date of its demise is not known, but : may have fallen into disuse during the First World War. The second course, on ground to the east of the village beside the River Awe, was opened in April 1935 by Major Bullough of Inverawe, whose speech was followed by an exhibition four ball match. This course closed when the Second World War roke out. The third course was laid out on much the same ground that the first course appears to have occupied. It was purchased from the Airds Bay state and was ready for an opening ceremony performed in 1991 by Michael Bonallack of the Royal and Ancient Golf Club in St Andrews. Some trophies rom the 1930s were brought back to be played for on the new course.

Many more houses have been built since this photograph was taken in 1905, the bridge across the River Nant in the foreground has been improved an a substantial footbridge installed alongside. With Tighnambarr to its left, and Highfield and Lochnell Lodge to the right, the Church of the Visitation i second from the left of the group of four buildings lined up across the centre of this picture. The church was built in 1901/02 to meet the spiritual need of the Catholic population. This was not large in an area where the influence of Clan Campbell was strong, but people attracted to the locality to work i the granite quarries had boosted the numbers. Prior to that, following the Reformation of 1560, people who remained Catholic had been restricted i property ownership and where they could meet by a series of intolerant laws. These only started to be superseded in the late eighteenth and earl nineteenth centuries clearing the legal obstacles to the building of churches.

Industry came to the Taynuilt area in 1752/53 when Richard Ford and Company came to an agreement with Sir Duncan Campbell of Lochnell allowing them to set up an ironworks. The company was already established in the Furness area of Cumbria, but in those early days iron was smelted using charcoal and the extensive woodlands of Argyll offered a more abundant source of fuel than could be obtained in the southern Lake District. Charcoal was a brittle material, easily damaged by rough handling and so it was better to bring the iron ore to the woodlands, than the other way around. Charcoal burning was carried out in the woods where trees were coppiced so that they could regenerate and produce a continuous supply of wood. The fire was controlled so that it did not consume the wood, but instead drove out moisture to leave a carbon-rich combustible material. In the furnace this burned at high temperature, bolstered by the blast of bellows worked by a wheel driven by water led from the River Awe. The furnace is seen here early in the twentieth century.

At the base of the furnace was a casting house where the molten iron was tapped and run off into a channel made of sand. This ha a number of smaller channels leading off it known as pigs and th iron cast in these was known as pig iron. There was no foundry a Bonawe, so these pigs were shipped back to Cumbria where the were used to make finished iron products. Output from the furnac began to decline in the 1830s, coinciding with the rise of the grea hot-blast furnaces of Scotland's central belt, which used coke o splint coal to produce huge quantities of iron from local ironston The small, technologically inferior, charcoal-burning furnace struggled to compete with these behemoths and after years o unequal struggle and intermittent working, operations ceased i 1872. These three pictures show the furnace in a dilapidated sta in the 1960s, not long before it was refurbished as an ancien monument and added to the area's list of tourist attractions.

lthough the pig iron was sent back to the foundry in England, the furnace did make raw iron cannon balls, some of which are believed to have been sed at the Battle of Trafalgar in 1805, hence the monument to Lord Nelson. The raw materials for the smelting operation were stored before use in large one sheds, which were built to the south of the furnace using construction techniques common in the Lake District. The buildings were carefully sited n ground that allowed the stored materials to be loaded into them at a high level and taken out at a lower level, thus saving a lot of lifting. Charcoal, or he coals' as it was known despite being derived from wood, was kept in the stores in the foreground of this picture. The building in the middle ackground was used for iron ore. It came from a variety of sources including carboniferous ironstone from central Scotland, local bog ore and haematite, red coloured ore from Cumbria. The miners who won it were known as the 'red men of Cumbria' because of the dust from the mines that clung to their cin and clothes.

The iron company built a stone pier on the east side of Airds Bay. Known as Kelly's Pier after the works manager, it was used to ship in ore and take ou the pig iron. Bark stripped from trees prior to the charcoal burning process was also shipped out for use in the tanning industry. Loch Etive was hazardous body of water to get in and out of because boats had to pass through the narrows at Connel where the dramatic Falls of Lora roar over a underwater rock ledge when the tide is ebbing. Safe passage can be made at high tide, although even then surface turbulence can throw a boat about bit, which must have been unnerving for the men working the sail-driven craft that served the iron works. The pier was also handy for other vessels an the contractors building the railway used it to bring in materials and supplies, although one vessel carrying rails foundered at the entrance to the loch i 1878. The pier, with the addition of a timber end section, is seen here early in the twentieth century.

When the furnace was set up there were few if any local men who could operate it, so most of the skilled ironworkers came from England. They needed housing, which was built by the company in two distinct ranges. The earliest (top left) was a row of eight one and half storey cottages, known locally as the 'top houses' and these were followed by the 'low houses', an L-shaped block of tenements. Inevitably this was not enough for all the company's employees and some had to find housing wherever they could. The people who lived in the foundry houses were allowed, like crofters, to keep animals and grow food, although the company also ran a store where its workers could obtain meal and other commodities as part of their wages. As these pictures from the 1960s show, the company houses remained occupied long after the works ceased to be operational. The manager's house, Bonawe House, was an altogether grander three storied mansion set in wooded grounds to the east of the works.

Inverawe House is a mansion of uncertain date although there may be an early laird's hou at its core. Held by a succession of Campbells since the seventeenth century it was sold in 19 to a new owner who engaged the architect Sir Robert S. Lorimer to redesign the interior, ar it was further modified externally in the 1950s. There was a bigger change to the wider esta in 1963 when the Inverawe hydroelectric power station was built to the north of the house. was designed to generate 100 million units of electricity annually using water fed through three-mile long tunnel, 23 feet, six inches in diameter, from the barrage across the River Av in the Pass of Brander (see page 8). A fishery and visitor centre was established in 19 between the power station and Inverawe House. The occupants of the house were able to tai fish from the river which they did using a cruive, a salmon trap, which is seen in the ear twentieth century picture on the right. It was situated just upstream from the house beside tl Clay Pool, a section of river much favoured by anglers.

oted for producing more, big heavy fish over such a short length than any other river in the country, the Awe was regarded with, well, awe by anglers. ne of the most celebrated catches was a fish weighing 54 pounds landed by the local schoolmaster. He hooked it about a mile above Inverawe and fought a epic battle, at one point wading through water up to his chin – and he was a tall man. He brought his prize ashore from Crubeg, the lowest pool on e river, beyond which the fish would have escaped into the loch. The river was, in angling terms, split into about thirty pools with names like the rander Pool, the Verie Pool, the Oak Pool, Casan Dhu, and Garravalt. At some of these, where the salmon lies were too far out for the angler to get to, on brackets were fixed to large boulders and, with wooden planks laid on these, the fisherman could reach the deeper water. It was precarious and pears to have been disused when this picture was taken because one of these brackets can be seen on the left, with water breaking around it.

There were two ferries at Inverawe. One linked the north and south shores of Loch Etive while the other took people across the wide mouth of the Rive Awe. This was important before the Bridge of Awe was built in the late eighteenth century because it got people safely to the east of the river dry sho and provided a crossing for people making their way along the loch shore. Although the river mouth was wide, there was still a strong flow, which mea that the rower had to make a wide detour upstream before guiding the little boat to the landing point on the opposite bank. Known in its day as th 'penny ferry', the fare had increased several fold by the time the service ceased around the early 1960s. The mouth of the river was also a prime spot f netting salmon. This was carried out over a longer season than was allowed for anglers, much to their irritation, but with prime fish being despatch by train to markets in the south the fishery was a useful source of local employment.

lean Duirinnis, the site of the northern slip of the Bonawe Ferry, is seen here in Edwardian times. The ferry was a vital link in the route that cut through e glens between Loch Creran and Loch Awe, saving many miles of hard slog for drovers and travellers on foot or horseback. Alasdair MacIain acDonald of Glencoe also came this way on his fateful journey at the turn of the years 1691 – 1692, when his late arrival at Inveraray was used as the retext for the massacre of his clan. Initially, large or small rowing boats were used, depending on whether animals or people were being carried, and a rry capable of carrying cars was introduced in 1914. The *Deirdre*, a vessel that could carry four cars, a bus or a ten ton lorry, was put on in 1937 by the en operators, J. & A. Gardner, who also worked the quarry. A new boat, the *Dhuirinish*, took over in the 1950s despite a 1948 Ministry of Transport nquiry into all British ferries making no recommendation for the future of the service. She carried on until 1967 when better roads, faster cars and free ccess to the Connel Bridge had ended the need for a Bonawe Ferry.

Bonawe Quarry is one of the most visible features of the Taynuilt area, despite being on the north side of Loch Etive. It was opened to work a sma
outcrop of fine grey granite, part of a complex of granites that make up Ben Cruachan and the surrounding hills. The main operators were the firm
J. & A. Gardner who leased it and two neighbouring quarries in 1892. In over a century of operations they created a huge scar on the face of Be
Duirinniss, and often woke the echoes when blasting was in progress – they did tend to go big when they went for a blast at Bonawe. The quarry's ma
products were chippings for road making and cobbled setts for paving city streets, but it also produced dressed stone for buildings and a vast quanti
of granolithic. The picture shows the little shelters beside the loch where men worked shaping the stone. In the background, on the Taynuilt side of th
loch, are the slopes of Ben Cruachan where the smaller Inverawe Quarry extracted a similar range of granite products to those won at Bonawe.

As well as operating the Bonawe Quarry, J. & A. Gardner owned a fleet of coasting vessels. Utilitarian rather than pretty, they were a familiar sight on the west coast and distinctive because of the broad white band around the black funnel. They were used for general cargo, but when none was available they went to the quarry to load stone, so they were never idle. One of these boats, the appropriately named *Bonawe*, is seen here at the quarry. Launched in October 1903 at the yard of Scotts of Bowling, on the Clyde, she weighed 242 tons and measured 117 feet long and 22 feet in the beam. She came to an untimely end in June 1917 when, on a voyage from Ayr to Larne with a cargo of coal, she collided off Arran with the Admiralty yacht HMY *Iolaire*. *Bonawe* sank, but Captain Hannah and his crew of six all survived. Eighteen months later *Iolaire* grounded on rocks while entering Stornoway Harbour and sank with the loss of 205 men returning to the islands after the First World War.

The whitewashed cottage, 'Granny's Heilan' Hame', is an emblematic image of Highlands, but this picture of a house at Airds differs from the usual prettified version because it shows the back of the building, not the front. The photographer has also allowed a barrel, cartwheels and other detritus to fill the foreground. There are some clues as to the way the house may have been used: the thatched roof appears neater on the left, above the window which suggests that at one time people lived in that half of the house while animals occupied the other. This was common practice, but the home-made looking chimneys sticking through the thatch might indicate that, when the picture was taken, the whole building, with an internal partition, was used for human habitation. This is conjecture and the reality will probably never be known, but with crudely ventilated open fires, an imperfect roof and minimal daylight, picturesque might have been as good as it got at this particular 'heilan' hame'.

Taynuilt may be surrounded by majestic mountains and rugged uplands, but the village is where it is because the rivers and burns that flow toward Loch Etive have, over millions of years, created a large patch of relatively flat land where, for centuries, people have been able to grow food and graze animals. This image of the wild highlander as a peaceable farmer may not fit the stereotype, but it was how people lived and they did so in small township communities like Airds, seen here in a picture from the early twentieth century. The ground close to houses was cultivated, the more marginal land beyond that was cropped or grazed and on the higher ground were the summer sheilings, where cattle could graze without damaging crops. Although the Crofters Holdings Act of 1886 gave tenants security of tenure, few townships survived the nineteenth century intact. Auchindrain on Loch Fyneside is the most complete example, but the clusters of dwellings at Taynuilt are echoes of what was once the typical way of Highland life.

Hafton, on the opposite side of the main road from Airds, is not a unique name to Taynuilt, because it is also applied to an estate near Dunoon and may have the same linguistic roots as Afton Water in Ayrshire, the 'sweet Afton' that Robert Burns famously implored to 'flow gently'. Whatever its origin (Gaelic, old Norse?), Hafton is seen here in a picture taken in 1913, just before the outbreak of the First World War. It was a time when such images of timeless countryside idyll were popular with a strand in society who thought that the long halcyon days of summer would go on forever. Those who had to wield the scythe and rake in the hay in hot sunshine probably thought they did go on forever! Taynuilt's early post office was located near here before it was moved closer to the railway station. In the distance, just to the right of centre, is the Muckairn Free Church, erected in 1860 following an event known as the Disruption.

In 1843 almost half of all ministers and an even higher number of parishioners left the Established Church of Scotland to form the Free Church. It was one of the biggest upheavals in Scotland and led to the redrafting of some significant aspects of social legislation such as the poor laws and education. At the core of the dispute was the power of the patron, often a landowner, who had the right to appoint a minister contrary to the democratic wishes of the congregation – a cornerstone of Presbyterianism. In Muckairn Parish a very high number of people followed their minister out of the church. As with many Free Church congregations they had to worship where they could and, for a time used a building attached to the ironworks, before their new church was built. The Presbyterian churches were reconciled in 1929 and the local congregations amalgamated soon after. No longer required as place of worship, the building was used for a time as a hall and was later converted for use as a private house.

Although the beach at Airds Bay is strictly speaking beside the seaside, it has never quite reached the levels of popularity enjoyed by Blackpool o Brighton. Such details were clearly of little concern to the people in this picture who appear to be enjoying a day in the sun beside Loch Etive. The da looks warm, as it can be in the west of Scotland, because the folk in the distance are shading themselves with a parasol. Some children are paddlin, although the optimist with a bucket might have found it tricky to build a sand castle out of the somewhat stony raw material. The kind of recreation popular with villagers have changed over the years, with more activity likely on the sports field than the loch side. Designed to be long enough for shint and wide enough to accommodate a football pitch, the field is also the venue for the annual Taynuilt Highland Games, one of the highlights of the yea

the background of the picture on the facing page are the houses clustered around the west side of Airds Bay. This little cottage, photographed in 1905, was one of the humbler of those dwellings; the biggest and grandest was Airds Bay House, the residence of the local landowner whose estate took in much of Taynuilt including the hotel where every year a room was turned into a temporary office to receive payments of feu duty, a form of land rental, om householders. A change to the law in the 1970s effectively ended the imposition of feus. Round stone gate posts, similar to those seen on the inside ont cover at Sandbank, flank the entrance to the road that connects this little enclave to the wider world. A track that led from the road around the bay the village crossed a ford over the Airds Burn close to where the boy in the picture was trying his luck with rod and line. The ford has since been perseded by a little bridge and some modern houses have replaced older buildings.

To the west of the houses at Airds Bay is an undulating area of naturally regenerating woodland known as Airds Park. Part of the Muckairn Estate, it i split by a burn that forms a little promontory with the shore where it enters Loch Etive. This idyllic spot is crowned by Muckairn Castle, an old laird' house extended and embellished in the Scots baronial style and seen here in a picture from the 1930s. Airds Park became legendary in the sport o orienteering when it was included in a week of events in August 1989. Competitors had come from all over the UK and Europe to run and navigate, wit map and compass in hand, over Scottish terrain. At Airds Park they found themselves in a bewildering landscape with no clear lines of sight and fe walls, paths or prominent features to help them re-orientate when they got lost. Heavy underfoot conditions also made progress tiring and man over-confident competitors were humbled that day in Airds Park.